Adoption i

Not Just foı u ~ıɔ

Ruth Layzell

Director of Counselling Training,
St John's Extension Studies, Nottingham

GROVE BOOKS LIMITED
RIDLEY HALL RD   CAMBRIDGE   CB3 9HU

Contents

The Cover Illustration is by Peter Ashton

First Impression March 1999
ISSN 0144-171X
ISBN 1 85174 398 7

1
Introduction

Until I became an adoptive parent myself, I would have said that my experience as a social worker involved with fostering and adoption made me something of an expert in the field. I had prepared children for placement and worked with them afterwards, had run preparation groups for prospective adopters and counselled adult adoptees wishing to trace their roots. But nothing really prepared me for what it was like when our children arrived. I was grateful for what I knew, but also began to recognize the limits of it.

If, as a professional in the field, my understanding of adoption proved so limited, it is likely to be much harder for the general practice pastoral carers in churches to keep an accurate perception of what adoption really means. The task is made more difficult because of the vast changes which have taken place in the ethos and practice of adoption in this country this century, and more difficult still because it is still not easy to talk about adopting, being adopted or relinquishing a child for adoption. The changing picture cannot then be reflected in the community story-telling which helps us stay in tune with each other.

Those with pastoral responsibility will no doubt come across adoption as a possible option for childless people or as a plan for children at risk, and being well informed in these circumstances will be essential. But beyond this, there are many people in our congregations who live with the complex impact of adoption and who—because so much has changed so quickly and professional understanding is still forming—can find themselves coping with things they had not been prepared for, behaving in ways they had not anticipated or feeling things they cannot account for.

I believe the Christian community is particularly well placed to support and care for all those involved in the experience of adoption. But in order to make good use of the resources it has to offer, the Christian community needs to have an accurate understanding of what it means to give up a child for adoption, to adopt or to be adopted. All too often, the experience of those most closely involved is that such understanding is lacking and so the pastoral care offered, while well intentioned, can miss the mark.

If Christians are to offer the companionship of those who are ready to share both tears and laughter, there is a need for better information. Only then can adoption realise its life-giving potential.

It is this need which I hope to address in this booklet. I shall describe the background to and some of the main issues in current adoption practice, outline the reality of the experience of those involved, as opposed to the myth, highlight what the pastoral task may be in relation to them, and reflect on the whole in the light of Christian faith, drawing out the life-giving potential in adoption. I shall illustrate my exploration by using my personal story and two fictitious case studies.

2
Historical Background

Although the practice of adoption has been a feature of many societies since an-
cient times, the British were reluctant to introduce it into legislation. The first
British adoption law was not passed until 1926 (see Triseliotis, 1998, pp 56–66)
when fears about the practice of adoption were outweighed by need to provide
legal security and recognition for the children—either orphaned or illegitimate—
of men who had fought and died during the First World War (Fratter *et al*, 1991, p
7). The number of adoptions at this point was relatively small (4,500 were regis-
tered in 1930) but had doubled by 1940. The number of adoption orders increased
again in the wake of an upsurge in out-of-wedlock pregnancies during and just
after the Second World War (14,000 orders in 1950) and continued to rise during
the sexual revolution of the sixties until it reached its peak in 1968 with 27,000
orders being made that year (Fratter *et al*, 1991, p 8). During the 1950s and 1960s,
adoption was used to 'regularize' arrangements for the upbringing of children.
Single parenting was socially unacceptable and often linked with poverty and so
the pressure was on unmarried women without financial means to relinquish
their babies so that largely middle class infertile couples could adopt them. During these decades, both adult parties to the adoption arrangement were protected
by strict rules about confidentiality. Both the law and adoption practice aimed to
create an impenetrable barrier between birth and adoptive families in the belief
that a 'clean break' was better for all concerned. The expectation of both adopters
and practitioners was that only children with a good background and little risk of
illness, disability or delinquency would be placed (Triseliotis, 1998, p 64). The
focus of adoption was to serve adults who wanted children and adoption would
not have been considered for older children, children with disabilities, black and
mixed parentage children, groups of siblings and children who had come into
care as a result of parental neglect or abuse. Such children would have been placed
in long-term foster care or children's homes.

The climate in adoption changed decisively during the 1970s (Fratter *et al*,
1991, pp 9–10). By this time, contraception was more readily available and abortion had been legalized. It was more acceptable for single women to bring up
their babies and housing and financial provision had been made for them. As a
result, fewer babies were becoming available for adoption.

However, the number of couples wishing to adopt remained constant, and it
became not only possible but also prudent for practitioners to think about adoption as a plan for the children who had previously been thought of as 'hard to
place.' At the same time, the 1975 Children's Act introduced the concept that any
decision-making in respect of children should consider the child's welfare as of
paramount importance, even where this conflicted with the needs or wishes of
the parents.The child's rights—particularly to continuity and security—were

emphasized, and policies which advocated permanency for children were developed in place of policies which largely reacted to parents' wishes. Adoption began to be seen as the plan of choice for a range of children who would otherwise have languished in children's homes or been shuttled back and forth between home and care.

In addition, as a result of research (Triseliotis, 1973) and pressure from adult adoptees, the Children Act 1975 for the first time allowed the strict confidentiality in which most adoption placements had been made to be breached. Section 26 of that Act gave adoptees, at eighteen, a right of access to their original birth records, and so to information about their origins. This irrevocably changed adoption practice from 1975. Adoptees could not gain access to their birth records without counselling from a specialist social worker and so for the first time adoption workers were meeting adult adoptees and could learn from their experience. This made systematic research into adoption feasible and the information gleaned from such studies has proved invaluable in developing improved policies and practice. In addition, both the relinquishing family and the adoptive parents needed to be prepared for the possibility that the adoptee would want information about his or her origins at the age of 18. For the first time, adoption workers began to prepare adopters for the task of talking to their children about adoption.

Adoption in Britain today is thus very different from adoption as it was practised even 20 years ago. In place of strict confidentiality is a greater degree of openness about a child's origins and life history, and parents are encouraged to keep an open dialogue with their children about this. As infant placements have become rarer and adoptions of children from care (who are usually older and have some memory of their history) have become more the norm, so issues of contact with birth families have begun to be considered routinely. This means that far from there being a complete cut off from previous history for the adopted child, some form of partnership may be envisaged between birth and adoptive family for the sake of the child. Adoption has changed from being primarily about solving adult problems of inheritance or infertility to being primarily about the needs of children who cannot be raised in their families of origin.

3

Adoption—Solution to Crisis or Lifelong Task?

Popular understanding has not kept up with the changes I have described. Where accurate information is missing, myth and misperception usually creep in and this is certainly true of adoption.

Perhaps the most common misperception is that adoption is a neat solution to a three cornered crisis: the crisis of parentless children; the crisis of childless parents; and the crisis of parents with children they do not want or cannot keep (Verrier, 1993, p 7). The solution, so the story goes, is to move everyone round one (like some statutory Mad Hatter's tea party) so that the children end up with the parents who want and can care for them, those parents end up with children and those who do not want or cannot provide for them end up with none—and everyone will live happily ever after (Miller-Havens, 1996, p 273). The trouble is that real life is not that neat, and the only way to make it so is to cut out the human emotion which messes it up. In real life, the story most often begins with the heartache of unfulfilled hope, unplanned disruption and unwanted trauma.

The Adopters' Story

'Married for five years, with two careers underway, in our late twenties/early thirties, as the biological clock ticked on, we began to think about having children. We had so far achieved our life plans. It never occurred to us that in this most basic of areas—our sexuality and reproduction—there would be a problem.

'But there was. Like many other couples, in spite of extensive investigation "the problem" was never identified and, in spite of various treatments, never overcome. The pregnancy we had hoped for never happened. The experience challenged our ideas of God as provider and healer and threw us back often to wondering if there was something we had done wrong to deserve this gnawing pain of unfulfilled longing. The baptism liturgy ("God is the creator of all things, and by the birth of children he gives to parents a share in the work and the joy of creation") which my husband, a priest, had to recite regularly during those years became particularly poignant and painful (why doesn't he give us a share in it too, then?) and Mothering Sundays were an ordeal. While my husband was at the front of church taking the service, at some point I would be weeping at the back.

'After five years of waiting and trying, we had lost hope of conceiving naturally and decided that we had had as much investigation and treatment as we could manage. We began to consider other ways of forming the family we longed for and our thoughts turned to adoption.'

A Birth Mother's Story

'I was 18 at the time. I'd been going out with Andy—the only man I've ever really loved—for over a year. We'd started a sexual relationship when we went to

6

university. We were usually very careful about contraception because neither of us wanted children. But one time we took a risk and I became pregnant. I was terrified. I had my future mapped out. I didn't want to stop my course and I didn't want the responsibility of a child at that stage in my life. Andy suggested abortion, but I couldn't face it and he supported me in that. We thought about getting married, but we both knew we weren't ready to settle down. My parents thought about how they could help me keep the baby. But they couldn't think what they could do practically with me living away from home so much of the time and I didn't want them to bring the baby up so that I knew him but wasn't his mum. No plan that we could think of seemed like a solution. In the end I decided to think about having him adopted. At least that way I would know that he had gone to a family who really wanted him.'

A Child's Story

'My name is Sally and I'm 14. When I was little, I lived with my mum and my gran at my gran's house. When I was 8, my mum met Gary. Mum got pregnant, so we left gran's and got a house of our own in another town. Gran was a bit of a weird lady, but I still think about her and wonder if she's OK. Mum and Gary got married and had my brother Tom. I was 9 then. Mum started talking and acting weird when Tom was born and she couldn't look after him, so Gary and me did everything. Mum was like that for a long time and Gary shouted at Mum a lot because he said he had to do everything. He didn't though, because sometimes he'd go out and leave me to look after Tom. I hated him being nasty to Mum. Mum got pregnant again when I was 11 and she got so bad she had to go to hospital. After Gemma was born, some people came to take her and Gemma to hospital and she screamed because she didn't want to leave me and Tom on our own with Gary. I think she knew that he had been touching me. When she was away he did it more. This time he really hurt me and I got scared. After a while I told my teacher. I didn't know that we would have to leave home, too. I just wanted it to stop. Jenny, our social worker, came and I had to talk to a police-woman. Then Jenny took me and Tom to Jane and Jeff's house. Later on, Gemma came to live with us, too. Jenny says we wouldn't be safe to go home because Gary says he didn't touch me and Mum isn't well enough to stop it happening. Really there's not enough room at Jane and Jeff's for all three of us, so Jenny is looking for a family where we can stay. I wanted to go back to gran's with Mum, but Jenny says gran is too old to look after us and Mum doesn't want to live with her anyway. Jenny thinks it will be better for Tom and Gemma to be adopted, but I don't know if I want to be because I miss Mum and I want to be able to see her sometimes. I want to be with Tom and Gemma, though. I'm glad I don't have to see Gary anymore. I wonder who my real dad is.'

These three stories show that even in the beginning of the adoption story there is a complex mix of need, loss, grief and ambivalence. Pastoral care which attempts to simplify the complexity by isolating one aspect of the mix will be likely to prove inadequate in supporting the different members of the adoption triad as they make the best decisions they can, adjust to circumstances beyond their control and seek to find a positive outcome in a less than ideal situation.

The reality that members of the adoption triad live with is that, far from being a simple solution, adoption is much more likely to 'complicate the lives of all those involved for the rest of their lives' (Watson, 1997).

The first complicating factor is that although one of the aims of adoption is that it should achieve something positive for all those involved, adoptive families come together because of three sets of losses: the adopted child's loss of their birth family; the adoptive parent's loss of biological children; and the relinquishing family's loss of a child born to them. These losses are subtle and, particularly where silence and stigma about adoption are marked, often covert. Each member of the adoption triad will need to grieve these losses over time, so that they can integrate the reality of their experience and find a way to move forward.

Secondly, it is in this atmosphere of loss that adoptive parents and adopted children will be forging the bond between them, 'a bond forged in the fire of sacrifice and pain, not the easy fluid continuity of bonding [a child] might have had with her birth mother' (Verrier, 1993, p xvii). The circumstances of the bonding make the task not impossible, but complex, and parents particularly have to work hard with their children for it to become secure.

Thirdly, adoption creates 'a new kinship network that forever links those two families together through the child, who is shared by both' (Reitz and Watson, 1992, p 11). This is also complex because the two families so joined in most cases would not otherwise know each other and might not choose to be linked. One family may have been judged by social workers to be unfit to parent and the other family will have been specifically approved to do so. Feelings between the two families may be highly ambivalent, in all likelihood a mixture of gratitude and envy, anger and compassion.

And finally, as Watson makes clear, adoption is not like the solution to a mathematical or mechanical problem, which once identified and addressed puts the situation right. Instead, the process of coming to terms with the events and losses which have led to an adoptive family coming together is work which will continue for all parties over a lifetime. Those who support prospective adopters or birth parents considering adoption need to have a clear perception of the reality so that they can give realistic information both about the potential benefits and the complications of adoption.

It is my belief that one of the challenges for the adoptive family is that it falls largely to them, with support, to hold together the complexity I have described above, in order to give their children the best chance of turning their losses to gain and so discovering the life-giving potential of their history. The adoptive family, in turn, will need a supportive community if they are to meet this challenge.

In the next sections, I will describe the losses which each member of the adoption triad has to work through in order to make a good adjustment to adoption before going on to describe the vocation of adoptive parenting in more detail.

4

The Birth Family

'I didn't know when I thought about having my baby adopted that I would become so attached while I was pregnant. At first, all I could think of was that being pregnant was getting in the way—of my studying, of my relationship with Andy and of the way I had thought my life would go. But as time went on, I found myself feeling much more mixed about the thought of what would happen after the baby was born. The social worker at the hospital was really helpful and I never felt pressured into deciding one way or the other. But deciding was very hard. You can't carry a baby inside you for that long and feel nothing. At the time I felt I just had to grit my teeth and get on with it, that it was the best thing for everyone, but caring for him for the first few days before he went to the foster home made it really hard to say goodbye. After I'd handed him over to the foster mother, I shut myself in the loo and sobbed. When my parents came to take me home, I put on a brave face but I felt empty and lost.

'I couldn't really talk much about it afterwards. I must have been very hard to live with. At times I would feel depressed and worthless; other times I'd get very angry for no reason and take it out on Andy or my parents. I'm sure it was my moods that meant Andy and I split up. I think the pressure was too much. I suspect he knew that giving the baby up was affecting me, but I couldn't talk to him about it. He never seemed to be that upset himself, so it didn't seem OK to show him that I was. And there wasn't anyone else I could really talk to either. People were sympathetic for a few weeks but once I was back at college, people thought I should get on with my life. That's what I'd wanted after all, but the effects of losing the baby stayed with me for a long time. The worst part was giving my consent for him to be adopted. I knew I would—it wouldn't have been right to upset his new family—but it was still difficult to do.

'I still think about him. I've thought of him on his birthday every year. Other things trigger it off, too. He'd be seventeen now—a young man. When I see boys his age, I think about him and wonder how he's doing. I haven't had any contact with his adoptive family, but I'm preparing myself for the fact that he might want to get in touch with me when he's 18. I don't know what I'd feel about it. Andy and I met up with each other again 5 years ago—after a failed relationship each—and we're back together. That's strange. I sometimes wonder if we should just have had a go at making a family in the first place...'

In many ways, it is the birth family's loss which is most obvious in the adoption triad: a child born to them is gone. Yet it has been the birth family's needs and feelings which have historically most easily been overlooked. As recently as the 1950s and 1960s, the dual stigma of conceiving a child outside marriage and of relinquishing a child for adoption meant that birth mothers felt that very little consideration was given to them. Adults who gave advice were likely to believe that having their baby adopted was the correct thing for unmarried women to do (Bouchier *et al*, 1991, pp 89-90) and mothers often experienced hospital and adoption agency staff workers as showing little interest in their feelings and reactions. 'The baby was their only concern' one mother commented (*ibid*, p 34). Some mothers found attitudes and actions to be judgmental and even punitive. 'Nobody came to tell me about the baby. I thought "he is not mine at all, I cannot even ask about him." It was as though you were being punished' (*ibid*, p 34). Parents' reactions varied from ashamed but supportive to those who completely disowned their daughter (*ibid*, p 29).

Though attitudes and practices have changed, Bouchier (1991, p 96) notes that parents who relinquish their child for adoption are still unlikely to be given the help and support they need. It is generally accepted that bonding between mother and baby begins in the womb and that parents who lose a child at birth are bereaved. This understanding has informed the way professionals deal with miscarriage and stillbirth, but is not so readily applied to parents who place their child for adoption. Perhaps, as in abortion, the choice not to parent a child you have conceived is still surrounded by censure and stigma. Yet the bond formed during nine months of pregnancy is just as much disrupted and parents have to grieve the fact that they will not be able to see their baby grow up.

In addition, the mother loses significance and control. When she was carrying her child, she was the focus and source of her child's life, but once the decision to relinquish is made, others take over the planning and care. Even if this is clearly the woman's choice, it is likely to be psychologically difficult to adjust to. Where she feels pressured into making a decision for adoption, the grief will be much more complicated.

Recent developments in grief theory (Klass, Silverman and Nickman, 1996) as well as research into birth mothers' adjustments to the adoption of their children (Bouchier *et al*, 1991) suggest that far from being a loss which is grieved and 'got over,' the loss of birth children for adoption is a grief which affects relinquishing parents over their lifetime. One mother commented: 'It is like a death but you cannot let the feelings die. They resurface at every stage' (*op cit*, 1991, p 58).

The mothers in Bouchier's study still felt 'the deepest bond' (*op cit*, p 108) with their children. They would include them in their everyday thoughts and try to imagine what they would be like or would be doing (*ibid*, p 112). Though parents who lose a child through death also grieve through the expected life trajectory of their children, parents who lose a child through adoption may keep alive a hope of reunion. This may make it more difficult to resolve adoption related grief. 'Where a person has died there is finality. In adoption, there is the knowledge that the adopted child is almost certainly still alive, and it may be impossible to hold the two opposing forces [of loss and hope] in balance' (Bouchier *et al*, 1991, p 113). Perhaps the difficulty in finding a place for their grief accounts for the overwhelming opinion of mothers in Bouchier's study that 'parting with a child for adoption results in significant emotional damage to every birth mother' (*op cit*, p 93).

Where a child is placed for adoption as a result of legal proceedings designed to protect and promote the long term welfare of the child, the loss for the parents and other members of the family is likely to be even more complex. Parents will have to face being judged to be inadequate or unsafe parents for their child. Loss of their child will also mean unchosen loss of control and many parents have to deal with the anger they feel as a result. They may have contested the plans for adoption or refused to give consent, either from a desire to retain control of their children's destiny or to show the children that they did not wish to abandon them. For all sorts of reasons, the likelihood is that, whether or not they are able to care for their children, these parents will feel a deep sense of attachment and the loss of them may be extraordinarily painful.

Grandparents, siblings and other members of the extended family also lose the child placed for adoption. Although they may understand the reasons for the adoption and be unable to provide for the child themselves, the loss may be felt keenly. Even when contact is envisaged and pursued, the nature of relationships within the kinship network are changed by adoption and these changes need to be grieved and accommodated.

Whether children are placed for adoption with or without parental consent, those involved with the relinquishing family need to be aware that they are bereaved and need the same kind of support as those grieving following a death. Perhaps Christian pastoral carers may have something particular to offer in crafting a rite of passage for those experiencing this form of bereavement.

5

Adopters

'Before I could think of adoption as a way of making a family, I needed to let go of the hope of becoming pregnant. In one sense there is no end to infertility, but I reached the point when I felt exhausted by the constant cycle of hope and disappointment and I wanted an end. But letting go of the hope of biological children proved immensely difficult and I needed the help of the counsellor I had been seeing in order to move on. I sat on the floor of her room one afternoon and worked my way through her tissues as I wept for the children I would never have. I was inwardly tussling with wanting to hold on to these children, even to the hope of them, and needing to let go. Then, quite suddenly, I was ready. I placed the soggy mass of tissues which had absorbed my tears on to the floor, relinquished my hope and offered my grief to God. I had let go.

'The decision to adopt took a while even after that. We talked about the possibility, about the sort of children we were thinking of (and found our ideas to be remarkably and reassuringly similar). After we applied to an agency, it took some time for statutory checks to be completed and for us to start on the home study (a series of interviews with a social worker to check your suitability and to find out what sort of children you might parent well). We both found it a gruelling, though worthwhile, procedure—a bit like having an extended job interview in which no part of your person or life was shielded from scrutiny. Then the wait to know if we had been approved (anxiety provoking, even though our social worker was confident that we would be) and the wait to hear if we had been chosen as adopters for specific children. We were very conscious that this process paralleled the infertility investigations—we were dependent on others if our hope for parenthood were to be realized. We had to wait and trust—and pray.

'Finally we had a phone call from our support worker to say that we were being considered for two children and that their social worker was interested in meeting us. She was obviously excited. We were terrified. Could we start to hope or not? Did we dare? Suppose the social worker didn't like us when she met us? (I found myself tidying the house—the crazy desire to create a good impression). Suppose we didn't like the look or sound of the children? Could we afford to be choosy or turn them down? Would we be labelled as difficult and not be considered again? A mixture of reasonable and unreasonable questions, fears, fantasies...When we met her, we listened to the social worker (who clearly liked the children) and warmed to what we heard, but it wasn't till we were (eventually) allowed to see a photo that we really began to engage. There was something about the mischievous looks on their faces—these were real, definite individuals—and we wanted to meet them.

'Other meetings to go through—the adoption panel to consider the match between us and the children, the planning meeting to think about how we would meet them, meeting them, meeting their birth mother and brother. And the process of getting to know them. Finally everyone agreed that they and we were ready for them to come, and our children moved in.'

Because the advent of children is seen as a happy event, it is hard for those around adoptive parents to recognize that losses are an integral part of making a family in this way. Brodzinsky (1998, p 22) comments that the already difficult decision to adopt a child (difficult because of the high value given to procreation by society) is complicated by the fact that many adopt as a result of infertility.

Grieving Fertility

The first task of prospective adopters is to come to terms with 'the deeply personal and painful experience of infertility' and let go of 'biological parent identity' in order to take on the identity of adoptive parent (*ibid*). Grieving over infertility is not straightforward, however, for a number of reasons. Firstly, there is no one event which marks the loss which is felt. This means, secondly, that grief may be experienced over a long period of time, with no natural term to it and with repeated blows (each period, each failed treatment) adding to the sense of loss. Thirdly, it is an intensely private grief which, because of the personal nature of sexuality and reproduction, individuals and couples may not find it easy to discuss. This means that support from their social network cannot be easily accessed. Fourthly, because there is no tangible, physical person or object which has been lost, it is hard for those around infertile people to recognize and therefore validate their loss. The lack of external validation makes it more difficult for the infertile to feel entitled to their grief and this in turn may inhibit expression of it. Lastly, there are no rites of passage to help infertile people acknowledge their loss and find ways of integrating it, unless, as in the example above, a personal ritual is found.

In spite of the difficulty in coming to terms with this intangible yet very real loss, it is vital that prospective adopters should do so. 'Although it is unlikely that infertility is ever completely resolved, it is important for the individual or couple to find a comfortable way of incorporating this painful loss into a healthy and functional sense of self' (*op cit*, p 24). If adoptive parents are still struggling with feelings of shame or low self-esteem, they may feel unworthy to become parents at all and will have less to offer a challenging adopted youngster than those whose sense of self is robust. If a couple have not recognized and worked through the impact of infertility on their relationship, they will present a vulnerable target for the adoptive child whose strategy for testing out the security of a new family is to play one parent off against the other.

Because infertility is a state which is only taken away by the conception and birth of a biological child, the grief of infertility cannot be resolved by adopting. Indeed, during the course of adoptive parenting, this particular grief is likely to come up again, and where observers expect joy, adopters may experience pain. I found the early days of adoptive parenting paradoxical: it was at the moments of most fulfilment in parenting my children that the grief of my infertility also hit me afresh. On one of these occasions I wrote: 'How I've longed and waited for such moments. Strange that in the having, I grieve for the not-having. I'd known that I was missing; now I know what I was missing.' It was as if the grief of infertility did not have a shape until my children gave it one—and then I could weep more effectively. Similarly, there are times in parenting them now when both they and I are, sometimes painfully, aware that they are not the children I would have given birth to had I been able to. There are times when they want attributes of mine that they believe they might have had if they had been born to me and there are times when both they and I long for their lives to be less complicated and we fantasize that everything would have been simpler had they been born to me. There will be times, too, in the future—for example, if they become pregnant and give birth—when my own grief may present itself again.

The experience of infertility, then, though it cannot be resolved, needs to be integrated in a way which supports rather than hinders the bonding of adoptive parents with adoptive child. Adopters must grieve the children they were not able to have in order to value in their own right the children they do have.

Apart from this initial loss which adopters face, there are others which surface in the process of their adoption application. The first of these is loss of control. In order to become adoptive parents, applicants must seek help and rely on others in a much more marked way than is true of biological parents. Brodzinsky (1991, p 24) comments that this loss of control can increase the anxiety and undermine the self-confidence of prospective adopters.

In addition there is a loss of predictability. For biological parents, once conception occurs, there are approximately 9 months in which to prepare and plan for the new arrival and to make the psychological adjustment to their new identity as parents. Adoptive parents can have no such confidence in predicting either the timing or the outcome of their waiting. After years of waiting to conceive, they undergo a similarly uncertain wait for an adoptive child to be placed with them, again increasing anxiety and undermining self-confidence (*op cit*, p 25). The transition to parent identity may have to be made quite quickly, too. Where, as in our case, the children are already talking and choose to call parents 'mummy' and 'daddy' soon after meeting them, the adults themselves have to get used not only to thinking of themselves as 'mummy' or 'daddy' but to referring to their partner by their new 'name,' too.

There may also be loss of status if comments (some unthinking, some intended to be supportive) indicate that adoptive parenting is second best—a consolation prize for not being able to conceive. Such comments may give rise to some anxiety in adopters about whether they will be able to establish a secure, loving relationship with an adopted child (*ibid*).

Incredibly, in spite of all the stresses outlined above, research has shown that the majority of adoptive applicants handle the transition to parenthood quite well (Brodzinsky and Huffman, 1988). Perhaps the process involved in becoming adoptive parents is not a bad test of whether individuals or couples have got the stamina and emotional resilience to engage with the complex package of parenting tasks which lie ahead of them! Nonetheless, in the absence of more empowering methods of assessment, those offering pastoral care to prospective adopters need to be aware of how anxiety-provoking and disabling the process may be and of the need for affirmation and reassurance. The uncertainty of the timing may mean that adoptive parents experience the final placement of their children as a profound shock. If so, they will be unable to take initiatives in asking for the support they need. Of most help in the early days will be

- offers of practical help (for me this came in gifts of good condition clothing and equipment and the occasional meal cooked for and brought to us)
- companionship (people coming to see you because they value you and like the children; the children being invited to tea or to play)
- unbidden gestures of solidarity (like the giant cookie one family brought to share with us on the day our children moved in)
- communication (people who care about you ringing up to see how you are—please do not leave us alone with this)
- genuine interest and delight in the children.

Like people in the early days of bereavement, new adoptive parents may need so much that they have not got the energy or the courage to keep asking.

6

Adoptee

'We've been at Jane and Jeff's for nearly a year now. I had to go to court and say what Gary did to me. I didn't like that because Gary says I am lying. But Jenny said I did really well and that it helped her make plans about where me, Tom and Gemma are going to live. Sometimes I'm sorry I ever said anything. It's made life so complicated. But I didn't want it to keep happening and I didn't want it to happen to Gemma. Jane says it might even have happened to Tom. Mum and Gary have split up and Mum's living where people can look after her. I see her about once a month—Jenny takes me. Sometimes the kids come too, but not always. Mum's really unhappy and I don't always know what to say. I think she'd be happier if we lived with her, but Jane says she can't look after herself, so she couldn't look after us, though she loves us very much. I want to look after her, but Jenny says I'm not old enough.

'Jenny's found a family who want to adopt us. It's taken a long time. I think it's good because Tom and Gemma are only little and they need a mum and dad who can look after them till they're grown up. They haven't really known Mum that much, so I don't think they'll worry how she'll feel about it, like I do. I don't know what I want for me. Jane's met them and she thinks they're great. But I don't want to say goodbye to Jane and Jeff. It was hard coming to live with them at first, but I've got used to them now. I don't want to get to know someone new. Tom and Gemma could go and I could stay with Jeff and Jane. Jenny says these people would be OK about visiting Mum sometimes, so I don't suppose they'd mind me going to see them. I'd want to know the kids were all right. But I don't know if Jane and Jeff want me to stay…'

'To hear adoptees mentioned in the context of loss or bereavement may seem inappropriate to some. Most would concede that, leaving aside the unusual case of the adoptee whose biological parents have actually died, a child who was relinquished or taken from parents in toddlerhood or later might legitimately be seen as bereaved in some sense, but what about those who were placed in the first weeks or months of life with adoptive parents? Do they not have real parents in their adopters? And how important is their connection to the parents they never knew, and who may never have acted toward them in a parental capacity?' (Nickman 1996, p 258)

A number of theorists argue that it is relevant to think of loss in relation to all adoptees, whether adopted at birth or later. As I noted above, it is well accepted that attachment or bonding begins between parents and child before birth, and that babies are as much primed to bond with their birth mothers as birth mothers are to bond with them. On the basis of this, Verrier (1993) has argued that infants taken from their mothers at birth suffer what she calls a 'primal wound'—the trauma of being separated from the only person they have ever known. Following Mahler (1975), she contends that young infants are psychologically unable to distinguish between themselves and their mother. What happens to the mother, happens to them; what happens to them, happens to the mother. Separation from the mother not only feels like the death of the mother but also the death of the child's vulnerable, emerging self (*op cit*, pp 30-32). Verrier (1993, pp 20-21) argues that in ideal circumstances, an infant needs the presence of the woman who carried him in the womb to help him to deal with the trauma of birth itself and that separation from her, whatever the circumstances, constitutes a trauma which, though not consciously remembered, is remembered in the psyche and cells (*op cit*, p 15). Many people adopted as infants, without knowing why, have a difficult time on their birthdays (*ibid*) and may have a deep feeling that a part of themselves is missing. For some this will be part of the motivation to search for their birth mother in later life (*op cit*, p 33).

Children moved later, after about 6 months of age, when they are able to differentiate between their mother and other adults are more likely to show fear and distress when moved from one caretaker to another (Fahlberg, 1988, p 22). It is then clearer to adult observers that they experience some form of loss, though again, infants do not have the cognitive ability to understand or integrate it.

Nickman (1996, p 258) expands the theme of adoptee loss by showing that, whether or not one is convinced by arguments such as Verrier's, loss can be seen to be an appropriate way of understanding adoptee experience 'when one broadens the concept to include loss that is recognized retrospectively.' He argues that though adoptees who were placed as infants or young children may not have the cognitive ability to recognize their experience as loss, as they gain that ability, so they recognize and can grieve the loss which has already taken place.

Brodzinsky (1998, p 30) comments that, especially for children placed as infants, it is during the primary school years (usually from the age of 6) that children first begin to think of their adoptive experience as involving loss: 'With time, this sense of loss can become quite profound, although subtle and not always observable to the outsider. There is the loss of birth parents, birth siblings and extended birth family; status loss associated with adoption-related stigma; loss of cultural, ethnic and racial heritage; loss of genealogical connections; loss of stability within the adoptive family; and loss of identity.'

For the adopted child, dealing with this cluster of losses is a complicated process which cannot be separated either from their environment or from their development in other respects. First, their experience of loss will depend on the age at which it actually occurred. Similarly, their expression of all these losses will vary according to the range of options at their disposal—and this will be determined both by their developmental stage and by their circumstances at the time. (How much permission is given for grief in the family in which they are living? How safe is it to express such feelings? How permanent do they feel their current carers are?) In addition, their capacity to understand and appreciate loss must develop over time as their conceptual ability grows. How far they are able to understand and integrate their losses will depend on how much information is available to them about their life and how far they are supported in the process of making sense of it. It is accepted that grieving over loss is a process which unfolds over time, but for children whose losses began early in their life history, the process will inevitably be prolonged because of their growing ability to appreciate what has happened to them. Brodzinsky and his colleagues (1998, pp 40-42) show that it is in the school years, until mid-adolescence, that adopted children present most behavioural or psychological difficulties. They surmise that this is because it is during these years that they are doing most work in realizing what has happened, making sense and adjusting to it, though they also comment that 'for both parents and children, the adjustment to adoption will be a lifelong process, with new tasks and challenges emerging at each stage of the family life cycle' (*op cit*, p 33).

This means that those who find themselves in pastoral relationships with adopted people need to recognize that adjustment to adoption is a lifelong task. In the light of what I have described above, comments that an adopted youngster 'can't always be looking back at the past' but must 'be grateful for what she's got now and get on with her life' are neither realistic nor helpful. Those who come alongside adopted youngsters in school, church, Sunday school or youth groups need to remember that these children are only able to make sense of their experience in stages, as they themselves mature. Indeed, it may not be until adoptees reach adulthood, marry and have children of their own, that some issues can be integrated. Adoptees will then need people alongside them who are not fazed by the time lag between events and the expression of feelings which relate to them.

7

The Vocation of Adoption

Having described the losses involved for all members of the adoption triad, and the unfolding work of grieving them, it may be that the picture painted so far seems rather gloomy and the lurking question may be: Why does anyone do it? The answer must be that there continue to be parents who are unable to provide for their children (Bouchier *et al*, 1991, p 114) and adults, unable to conceive, who are drawn towards adoption. Christians who consider adoption will want and need to address the question of whether parenting is part of their vocation—part of the purpose of their lives under God—and whether, often through the hard experience of their infertility, God may be calling them to become the parents of children who would otherwise not have a family.

If adoptive parenting may be thought of in this way—as a vocation—what kind of vocation is it? And what biblical themes may Christian people use to help them understand it?

Covenant

The first challenge which adoptive families face is that of making a secure family in a society which still places a high value on blood ties and is correspondingly less understanding and supportive of families made in other ways. How firm and how secure can a family be which is made, not on the basis of biological bond, but as a result of the failure of the usual ways of becoming family—both for parents and children—and on the basis of the choice of the parents to welcome and love a child conceived and borne by others?

Here, I believe, the Christian gospel has much to say. For at the heart of it is the covenant choice of God to make a people of his own. The biblical narrative talks of the birth of creation and of the first intimate, seamless bond between God and humankind. But it also talks of the failure of what God intended as humankind draws away from intimacy with God into self-seeking and self-involvement. The first, easy, bond with him is disrupted and humankind has been estranged ever since. Though there are clearly differences, there are also points of contact with the adoptive family which is also made as a result of the failure of natural processes.

The narrative goes on to show that, in spite of the failure of this first bond, God so desires relationship with humanity that he takes the initiative to restore and heal, first in his covenant with Abraham and decisively in the covenant made through the redeeming work of Jesus. Those who were not his people have been made his people (Hos 1.8, 2.23; 1 Peter 2.10), not as a result of a natural course of events, but by the choice and purpose of God (Jn 1.12–13). Paul specifically uses the imagery of adoption to describe the action by which God brings human beings into the status of co-inheritors with Christ (Rom 8.15–17). Interestingly Paul

18

sees both Jews (Rom 9.4) and Gentiles as the adopted children of God, and high-lights faith in the promise of God, not bloodline, as the hallmark of family membership (Rom 9.6–8). Only Christ, as the only begotten Son of the Father, has any right of inheritance. We, whose nature and origin is different, depend entirely on God's choice in order to share the benefits of his life. We enter his family by adoption.

Here, then, is the ground for hope for the adoptive family. The implication of the biblical narrative is that bonds may be made, not only through natural processes, but also through covenant, as one party commits themselves, through promise, to the wellbeing of the other. This is a bond made by choice, in which desire and need weave together to make the relationship. In the covenant, the one with resources dedicates them to the service of the one who needs them and in the process both are enriched.

I want to suggest, too, that the covenant between God and his people forms a model for the relationship between adoptive parents and their children. In the covenant God makes with humankind, it is his desire which initiates, his love which infuses and his strength which sustains the relationship. His part is to make and remain faithful to his promise. Ours is to trust that the promise will be made good for us. In adoption, it is the adopters who make the promise to be parents to children who have already suffered and the adopters who bear the burden of responsibility in the relationship. It is their desire to become parents which initiates the family, their love which must bear the burden of the losses which both they and their children bring, and their strength which must sustain the relationship. In contrast to the way adoption has been viewed in the past, it is not the children's responsibility to help the adults but the adults' responsibility, as a result of their choice, to nurture their children.

Yet bearing the burden of the losses and sustaining the relationship may prove no small task. Both children and parents bring into the family their history of loss—some of it known and some yet to be encountered. It is as the members of the family live together that hitherto unrealized losses are made real and need to be grieved. This may well mean that there is a fair degree of ambivalence about being in this family as the previous relationships or losses are grieved ('I want my other mum or dad or gran and if it weren't for you I'd have them'). Yet it is in the context of this family that these losses and traumas have to be worked out. The adoptive family becomes the crucible in which potentially disabling past experiences may be transformed into something usable for the children and it is the task of the adoptive parents to hold the boundaries of the family so that it is a safe place to heal and to grow.

Becoming Pain Bearers

I believe that part of the vocation of adoptive parenting is the willingness to become what Cotter (1990, p 17) has called 'pain bearers.' Again, our model in this is the God of grace who, in Christ, became flesh and shared our life 'in the raw' in order to redeem and transform it.

In the vocation of adoption, painbearing involves firstly an attitude of unconditional love and good will towards the children one has chosen to adopt. Adopted children, as others who have experienced loss or trauma, have a great capacity to feel that if bad things have happened to them it is because they are bad (Verrier, 1993, p 59) and feeling rejected or unloved has the same effect. Learning that love can be steadfast regardless of standards of behaviour is an essential step for children in healing this negative view of self.

Another aspect is helping children understand and interpret their experience. As they become more aware of how families are usually formed (usually beginning around the age of six—Brodzinsky, 1998, pp 29–30), they encounter the question: 'Why didn't my birth parents keep me?' and alongside the possibility that there is something wrong with them ('I'm bad, ugly, unlovable, difficult, too naughty,' Verrier, 1993, p 84) is the thought that there is something wrong with their birth parents (they were bad people—because how could any good person give their child away or let them go?). Both these thoughts are threatening to the child's emerging sense of self and without further interpretation would lead towards a negative self-image.The adoptive parents' task is to create an environment in which it is possible for their children to make sense of their experience 'in a way that is consistent with the child's best capacities for growth' (Nickman, 1996, p 272)—even where this means putting aside their own gut feelings and interests (*ibid*, p 269)

Painbearing also involves recognizing that all adopted children have suffered in some way, though the nature of this suffering and awareness of it will vary from individual to individual and will unfold over time. Alongside this is a willingness not only to be close when children are settled and content but also to stay close as they begin to encounter and express their suffering—close enough to feel the pain of it reverberating through one's own person.

Straightforwardly, this will mean parents being willing for the impact of the children's experience to hit them so that they can offer them the empathy they need. More complex is allowing children to grieve wholeheartedly for what they have lost, even when parents wish they did not or are glad they are out of an abusive situation. Hardest of all are those situations when children throw their pain at the parents because they have no other way of understanding or expressing what has happened to them. They may test out the security of this new family and their theory about being bad by giving them very challenging behaviour to handle. They may reproduce the conditions of the previous family as a way of remembering what it was like, and adoptive parents may be left feeling that they are being given a part to play which they do not understand and certainly do not want. They may throw the anger that belongs to the birth family at the adoptive parents because there is nowhere else they can safely work it out (Verrier, 1993, pp 56, 97). They may show adoptive parents what they feel by making *them* feel that way (for example, if children feel helpless, they may behave in such a way as to leave the parent also feeling helpless—*ibid*, p 97). The parents' task in all this is to be big enough to contain the complexities and contradictions of the children's experience—even to feel the chaos of it—in order to transform the raw experience into something which the children can digest (Rosenthal, 1996, p 170).

But for adopters, particularly in the current climate, the task is complex and apparently contradictory. Adoptive parents are simultaneously asked to make a firm bond with their children while keeping open dialogue about or contact with the birth family. They are asked to give accurate information about children's history while remaining compassionate towards the birth family and conscious of the tendency of children to think badly of themselves. They are asked to bear their own pain without passing it on to the children and to bear not only the children's pain, but also—because they live with the children—the consequences of the birth family's pain. There is a sense in which this is not fair, and yet it follows from the choice which adoptive parents have made.

In this, again, they are called to follow the way of Christ.

'We come to the deepest mystery when we see in the suffering of Jesus a disclosure of the suffering of God…What Jesus reveals on the cross…is the love which does not shirk suffering, and that love is God himself at work…The cause of Jesus' suffering is sin and the human predicament. He meets the situation by bearing what has to be borne that the work of love may get done. God in Jesus Christ suffers with his world, not meaninglessly, but redemptively'
(Williams, 1968, pp 185–86)

As the suffering of Jesus was undeserved but freely chosen in a movement of love, so the undeserved painbearing of adoptive parents is taken on as a consequence of their choice to open themselves to their children. Within the concept of covenant outlined above, 'those of larger size [and greater power] must undergo greater suffering and bear a greater burden' (Loomer, 1976, p 28) in order to sustain relationships which may contribute to the healing of past hurts.

All of the above implies that one task for the adoptive parents is to hold out hope for their adopted child. The difficult experiences of the past might draw children towards mistrust, depression and despair. Adoptive parents are called to hold out hope, not on the basis of a denial of what has happened in the past, but on the basis of trust in the the transforming power of the God of resurrection.

Adoption is for Life

I have majored, in the last section, on the way in which adoption may hold out hope for children. But the life-giving potential of adoption, the potential for redemption, is wider than this. For as they help their children to make sense of their experience and see them transform it into something useable, adoptive parents also experience transformation. The desire to nurture and invest in children, which was thwarted by infertility, finds its expression in relationship with these children, and their own experience of loss and unexplained suffering—though different from their children's—can nonetheless be put to positive use in empathizing with and supporting them through theirs.

Although this part is complex, adoption may also prove to have its life-giving aspects for birth families. Most obviously, if the adoptive experience works well, relinquishing families may have the relief of knowing that their children were well cared for during their childhood, in a way which they themselves could not manage. Further, if the adoptive parents do manage to hold the contradictions and tensions of adoption within themselves, and maintain a compassionate and open view of the birth family, children who may have tended to feel angry or vengeful towards relinquishing parents may come to a new understanding of their history, which allows for compassion and forgiveness.

8

Resources—the Life-giving Potential of the Christian Community

It will be apparent by now that my view is that adoptive parenting is not a vocation that should be undertaken lightly, for it is a demanding and life-long responsibility which will involve the parents not only in tasks shared by all parents, but in additional ones besides. This in turn means that adoptive parents need particular resources—both within themselves and in the support structures around them.

Inner resources will be to do with having encountered and worked through enough of their own loss and pain to be able to stay alongside their children as they work out theirs. This means that parents need to know themselves well enough to know what their painful issues are and when they may need help in the future. It also means that they need a firm sense of who they are so that they do not get lost or knocked off balance in the turmoil of their children's feelings.

But if adopters are to stay grounded and sure within themselves at the same time as being open to their children's emotional turmoil, they will need adults outside themselves to act as points of reference for them and to contain them in their own distress so that they can go on containing their children in theirs. Adopters may have extended family members or friends who take on this role for them, and, at least in the early days of a placement, the family's support worker is likely to have this role.

But I want to suggest that the Christian community is also potentially a good place for this sort of support. In a society where nuclear families are often isolated from extended family, the family of the church may come into its own if we are aware of the need for it. This community can support by being concerned, by offering practical help, by listening, by holding in prayer and by acting as a point of reference for adopters who from time to time may lose their bearings on what is normal.

But another reason why the Christian community is a good place to support those who are raising adoptive children is that Christians, of all people, are well placed to understand the depth of bonds of love and affection which do not rely on blood lines, which encompass the failure of the natural order and the choice of love to renew, to heal and to redeem. Individual Christians are themselves the adopted children of God and the church is a family made up of people who are not naturally related to each other and yet, because of their relationship with God, are bound together by a bond which is deeper and more lasting than any natural family tie. In contrast to the stigma attached to adoption in other parts of society, the Christian community should be well equipped to honour and understand this form of family-making and so support those who are involved in it.

But it is their relationship with God which is the most important of all the resources available to Christian adoptive parents. The adoptive task as I have set it out is stretching and demanding, and adoptive parents, like other parents, with the best will in the world, will know themselves often to fail. There will be times when they are not enough for their children, when they cannot hold within themselves the contradictions and paradoxes involved in adoption. At such times, when the best we have has been offered and found wanting, it is the steadfast love of God for us (imperfect as we are) and for our children (in all the mixture of their experience) which holds us firm and gives us hope. For our trust is in a God who stands with us in our pain, and suffers too; who promises to bear it and transform it into something usable for us; who knows the truth about our limits and our capacity for failure and undertakes to redeem; who can bring joy out of pain and life out of death; and who promises to open to us the resources of his infinite love as we open ourselves to him.

9

Bibliography

Bouchier, P, Lambert, L and Triseliotis, J (1991), *Parting with a Child for Adoption* (London: BAAF).

Brodzinsky, D, Smith, D and Brodzinsky, A (1998), *Children's Adjustment to Adoption* (London: Sage).

Brodzinsky, D M and Huffman, L (1988), 'Transition to adoptive parenthood' in *Marriage and Family Review*, 12, pp 267-286.

Cotter, J (1990), *Healing—More or Less* (Sheffield: Cairns Publications).

Fahlberg, V (1988), *Fitting the Pieces Together* (London: BAAF).

Fratter, J, Rowe, J, Sapsford, D, and Thoburn, J (1991), *Permanent Family Placement* (London, BAAF).

Loomer, B (1976), 'Two conceptions of power,' in *Criterion 15*.

Mahler, M, Pine, F and Bergman, A (1975), *The Psychological Birth of the Human Infant* (New York: Basic Books).

Miller-Havens, S (1996), 'Grief and the Birth Origin Fantasies of Adopted Women' in *Continuing Bonds*, Klass, D, Silverman, P and Nickman, S (eds) (1996) (London: Taylor and Francis).

Nickman, S (1996), 'Retroactive Loss in Adopted Persons' in *Continuing Bonds*, Klass, D, Silverman, P and Nickman, S (eds), (1996), (London: Taylor and Francis).

Reitz, M and Watson, K W (1992), *Adoption and the Family System* (New York: Guilford).

Rosenthal, J (1996), 'Love is Lovelier the Second Time Round' in *Partners Becoming Parents* (London: Sheldon).

Triseliotis, J (1973), *In Search of Origins* (London, Routledge).

Triseliotis, J (1998), 'Adoption—evolution or revolution' in *Signposts in Adoption*, Hill, M and Shaw, M (eds), (1998), (London: BAAF).

Verrier, N (1993), *The Primal Wound* (Baltimore: Gateway Press).

Watson, K (1997), Unpublished paper given at a workshop for adoptive parents, Beeston, 10th May 1997.

Williams, D D (1968), *The Spirit and Forms of Love* (Harper and Row).

Further Recommended Reading
General

Jones, M (1987), *Everything You Need to Know About Adoption* (London: Sheldon).

King, A (1989), *Adoption and Fostering* (Marlborough, Wilts: Crowood Press).

The Birthmother's Perspective

Howe, D, Sawbridge, P and Hinings, D (1997), *Half a Million Women* (Post-adoption Centre).

Books for Prospective Adopters

Fahlberg, V (1994), *A Child's Journey through Placement* (BAAF).

Howe, D (1996), *Adopters on Adoption* (BAAF).

Jewitt, C (1978), *Adopting the Older Child* (Mass: Harvard Common).

For Adoptive Parents

Keck, G and Kupecky, R (1995), *Adopting the Hurt Child* (Pinon Press).

Mansfield, L and Waldmann, C (1993), *Don't Touch My Heart* (Pinon Press).

Ruskai Melina, L (1989), *Making Sense of Adoption: A Parent's Guide* (Harper Collins).

Books for Use with Adopted Children and Young People

Krementz, J (1984), *How it Feels to be Adopted* (London: Victor Gollancz).

Lidster, A (1995), *Chester and Daisy Move On* (London: BAAF).

Livingstone, C (1990), *Why am I adopted?* (New York: Carol Publishing Group).